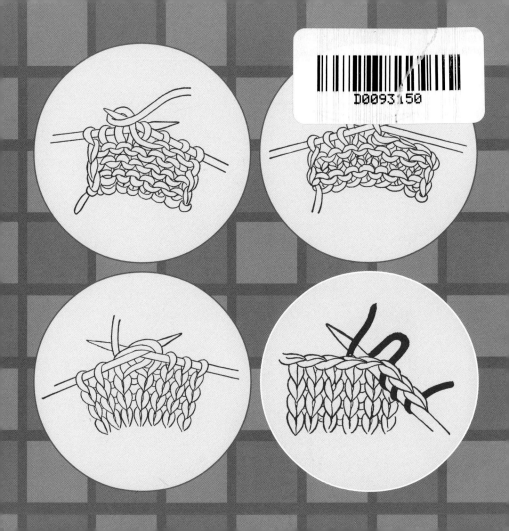

D0093150

In honor of the timeless allure of knitting

RALPH
PALLEN
COLEMAN

Knitticisms

. . . And Other Purls of Wisdom

Foreword by Kari Cornell

Voyageur Press

Edited by Michael Dregni
Designed by Maria Friedrich
Printed in China

05   06   07   08   09   5   4   3   2   1

Library of Congress Cataloging-in-Publication Data

Knitticisms— and other purls of wisdom /
[Edited by Michael Dregni] ; foreword by Kari Cornell.
      p. cm.
   ISBN 0-89658-707-X
   1. Knitting—Humor. I. Dregni, Michael, 1961-
II. Cornell, Kari A.
   TT820.K6947 2005
   746.43'2—dc22

                                        2004024719

Published by Voyageur Press, Inc.
123 North Second Street, P.O. Box 338
Stillwater, MN 55082 U.S.A.
651-430-2210, fax 651-430-2211
books@voyageurpress.com
www.voyageurpress.com

On page 1: A sweater design for a "glamour-minded rugcutter" from a 1930s pattern book.

On the title pages: Knitting at the beauty shop, from a 1937 *Home Arts Needlecraft* magazine.

Inset on the title pages: Knitting in Victorian days.

On the contents pages: Knitting that catches the eye, from a classic 1960s pattern book.

Inset on the contents pages: It's "sweatertime" around the clock, promises this 1950s pattern book.

Contents

BOOK No. 234 CLARK'S **ONT** · J. & P. COATS PRICE 10 CENTS

Learn to KNIT

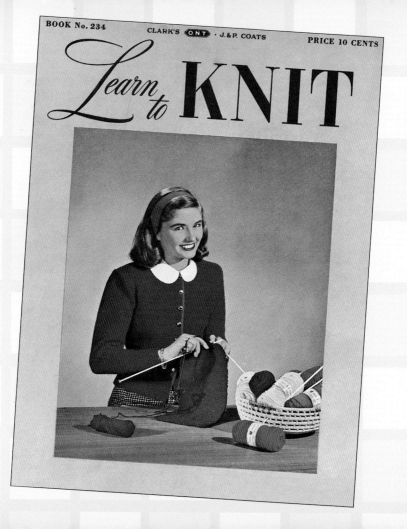

Knitticisms

By Kari Cornell

‒ ‒

Kari Cornell is a knitter who has learned the hard way to have a sense of humor about knitting. She's the editor of *For the Love of Knitting: A Celebration of the Knitter's Art*, also published by Voyageur Press.

‒ ‒

As anyone who's ever picked up yarn and needles with the intent of learning to knit will tell you, one of the most important attributes that all new knitters should have in their knitting arsenal is a sense of humor. After mastering the not-as-easy-as-it-looks art of holding the needles comfortably in one's hands and learning to knit and purl, the rest, it would seem, should be a piece of cake. But that's far from the truth. Trying to decipher the cryptic code of a standard knitting pattern is the next hurdle: Row 5: [P1, k1] 4 times, p3C6B, C6F, p3 [K1, p1] 4 times . . . Yes, the average knitter is faced with a bit of a learning curve when it comes to reading a pattern. Fortunately most knitting books include a key for translating knit speak into directions every neophyte is likely to understand. Then there's the math; math impaired beware. Creating the perfect fitting sweater will likely include a few calculations. But eventually, these challenges and others will all become second nature to the knitter.

Knitticisms
In learning to knit, a sense of humor is one key ingredient.

So why, then, is it so important to be able to laugh at yourself as you knit and purl down the path to a beautiful sweater, pair of socks, or cap? Because inevitably every knitter will make mistakes. Even the most seasoned veterans make errors, and one false move can add hours of additional work to a project.

Take, for example, my first official knitting project: a no-nonsense pair of mittens, to be knit in double-stranded mohair yarn—I selected an eye-popping spring green. In my naiveté, I didn't bother to check the gauge. Silly, silly me. I remember being most concerned about knitting with two strands of yarn, but that turned out to be a no-brainer. I gaily knitted and purled the fall evenings away, rocking in the vintage green vinyl rocker while my husband and I watched TV. I knit the mitts on 6.5 mm needles, so they took shape quickly, giving me an immediate sense of satisfaction. Before I knew it, I was binding off and stitching up the side seam of the first mitten. One down, one to go, I thought. I cast on for number two, not noticing that my gauge had relaxed as I became more comfortable with knitting and the pattern. Why I didn't hold the first mitten up to the second as I stitched to make sure the pair matched, I'll never know. You can see where this is going. I triumphantly finished the second mitten and pulled the first out of my knitting basket to show my husband. Oops. The second mitten would have been a better fit for a gorilla, while the first one fit me just right.

Hmm, what to do? It seemed silly to dismantle one of the mittens, stitch by agonizing stitch, as each seemed to stand on its own as a completed project. Instead I examined my stash. It looked as if I would have enough of the green mohair to knit one more mitten, so a third mitten there would be. Once

I completed it, I'm embarrassed to say that none of the mittens were a perfect match, but I was certainly getting closer! Maybe mittens, socks, and other garments that come in pairs aren't my thing. But at least I'll always have that third mitten, just in case I lose one of the others.

It is at moments like this when I thank the stars above for my sense of humor. And for books like this one, where fellow knitters who aren't afraid to poke fun at themselves and their knitting obsessions, relate their own mishaps and disasters with wit and grace. What better way to shrug off a knitting catastrophe than to snicker at the mistakes of others and, most importantly, realize you are not alone? So set aside your knitting needles and yarn (if only for a moment!), put your feet up, and read this fun collection of knitticisms page by laughable page. You'll be glad you did.

Learning to Knit
"Here's where the fun begins!" promises this 1940s beginner's guide.

Chapter 1

Much Ado About Knitting

How *Not* to Knit in Seven Easy Lessons

By Michael Dregni

Knitting didn't come easily for writer Michael Dregni,
but—despite problems with his gauge, tension, increases,
decreases, short rows, steeks, and math—he persevered.
Here he offers some hard-won purls of wisdom for neophytes.

How Not to Knit

Knitting lesson: For safety's sake, always wear the
proper knitting attire.

I learned to knit for all the wrong reasons.

Needing a new sweater, I decided to knit one. This was my first mistake—but far from my last. I should have walked the well-worn path to the store and bought that sweater: I would have had an instant choice of fiber, style, and color; paid a price cheap in comparison to knitting one; and been warm and comfortable there and then. Alas, my vain ambitions led me astray.

I tempted my innocent wife into teaching me to knit and, circular needles in my proud yet unsteady hands, began a downward spiral that continues to this day.

I offer my sad story as a morality tale for the unwitting at knitting.

Lesson 1
Abandon All Hope Ye Who Herein Enter . . .

I decided to make myself a simple black-and-white Norwegian Setesdal sweater, a traditional design in traditional colors. My wife sent me off to the knitting shop, and it was here that things went awry.

Crossing the threshold, I was an innocent drawn into the flame. For most men, yarn stores are foreign territory, about as inviting and exciting as a live bait shop or car parts store to the average woman. Instead of minnows or Rube Goldberg mechanical gadgets, there are overflowing shelves of multi-colored skeins and hanks of strange fibers culled from exotic animals like guanacos, funny-looking goats,

The Sweater Makes the Man
Knitting lesson: A well-crafted sweater says, "Light my fire!"

Knitting Blueprints
Knitting lesson: Consult your pattern early and often.

over-dressed rabbits, and grumpy musk ox. And instead of "Jake" in pungent, grease-stained overalls, there's a cabal of women in rainbow-colored sweaters speaking a foreign dialect peppered with phrases such as "steeks" and "stockinette" and thinking in pure cryptology like "K1, P1."

I bravely made my way past the curious looks and almost ran to a batch of black yarn, thinking I was safe. What I found instead was a display of novelty yarns—eyelashes, railroad ribbons, and funky furs. I spun around only to face a wall of frilly chenilles, handpainted variegateds, and super chunkys.

I panicked. Pink and poufy just wasn't me.

Then, fortune intervened and I was rescued. A woman who looked like central casting's perfect matron calmly asked if I needed help. Boy, did I ever. I explained my plans, and she led me straight to the collection of Peer Gynt yarns, ideal for my envisioned sweater.

I now realized that there was more than one "white" to choose from. Black was pretty basic, but there were bleached whites, off-white whites, natural and unnatural whites. My kind guide was unphased: She loaded my arms up with skeins. I was ready to begin knitting.

The moral of this story: Yarn is not yarn is not yarn.

Lesson 2
Knitting Mathematics

The second item of which virgin knitters should be warned is that knitting requires arithmetic, and if you scored "Trainable" on those childhood aptitude tests, you should think twice about venturing forth into knitting.

Spinnerin

GENTLEMEN PREFER

Knitting math seems simple enough. To knit a sweater body, one must multiple their own circumference by a vague and infinitely variable factor known innocently as "gauge." Your gauge is defined simply as the number of stitches of a certain yarn on a certain needle size that you knit per inch. And yet that number can vary depending on your mood, the weather, the chair you're sitting in, and, I have now come to believe, even the stars.

With my dear wife's helping hands, I knit a swatch to gauge my gauge. The first row went fine, but when I turned to purl back, I discovered something many knitters have also found: While my knit stitches were loose and even, my purls were as taut and tight as little square knots.

Swatching those first two or three rows took me two or three hours, and so I set my knitting aside for the night. When I returned the next day, behold, my stitches were looser as I became more comfortable knitting whereas my purls were even tighter as I became more adept.

My wife counseled patience, and I continued practicing until I measured my gauge at an average of six stitches to the inch on number 2 needles. Now I was ready to start the sweater body.

I spent the next week happily stitching away and by the weekend had knit my sweater up to my belly button. Proud of my handiwork, I showed it off to my wife. Her look was quizzical.

"Are you planning to gain weight?" she asked.

I examined my sweater body again and realized you could fit two

Knit Your Way into Her Heart
Knitting Lesson: Ladies prefer men in stylish homemade cardigans.

of me into it. At least. My gauge had become more relaxed as I became more confident, and when I wasn't paying attention, six stitches per inch turned into four. Except where I was doing two-color knitting and it shrunk back to six. And except where I returned to a single color without changing needle size and it blossomed back to four. My "sweater" would better serve as a hula hoop.

Moral: When it comes to knitting math, one plus one does not always equal two.

Lesson 3
As You Knit, So Shall You Rip

My next lesson was in ripping, a painful, cursed art that my wife taught me with what I sensed was a bit too much glee.

As my gauge had fluctuated so wildly, I simply had to start over, she explained with simple logic I simply didn't want to understand. When I hesitated further, she offered her assurance: Even the best knitters sometimes have to rip.

Still, it hurt. Pulling the needle out of those stitches was much more difficult than knitting them in the first place. In a melodramatic moment, each one seemed infused with my blood, sweat, and tears—B1, S1, T2.

Yet with all the patience of a mother guiding a child on its first knitting project, my wife cast out another "purl" of wisdom: To take a step forward, you sometimes first need to take a step backward. I ripped it all out and began again.

Moral: As long as you ultimately knit more stitches than you rip, you'll end up with a sweater. Eventually.

Movie Star Styling Knitting lesson: Clothes may not make the man, but a home-knit sweater could make you a Hollywood star.

Knits for the Links
Knitting Lesson: The right sweater can indeed improve your golf game.

BOTANY
HAND KNITS FOR MEN

No. 162

No. 154

VOL. 12
60¢

Lesson 4
Biting Off More Than You Can Chew—and Chewing On Too Large of a Bite

While I worked away with my miniscule number 2 needles knitting around an hour at best, my wife gaily finished her project. I realize I was a novice, but this just wasn't fair.

Watching her happily model her new creation, I attempted some more math. If my sweater was 40 inches around, each row required 240 stitches (depending on my elusive gauge). And if my sweater was 24 inches top to bottom at eight rows an inch, I needed about 192 rows. That totaled 46,080 odd stitches! I was going to be a couple years older before I too would be modeling my new sweater. And I probably *should* knit in some extra room around the belly to grow into.

Sensing my frustration, my wife let me in on a little secret: Big can be beautiful. Use a pair of number 18 needles—as big around as my forefinger—and you'll be snug and warm in your sweater before the snow flies.

Still, I was after that traditional look and a Setesdal with two stitches to the inch just wasn't morally right. I returned to my knitting and promised myself I wouldn't tally up stitches again.

Moral: The bigger the needles, the faster the results.

Lesson 5
If It Doesn't Unravel, You're Doing Fine

Several weeks passed and a sweater that might actually fit me began to take shape.

Still, something nagged.

When I examined my knitting closely, it just didn't look right. A run of stitches moved along merrily in fine, loose knit—only to be interrupted by the odd single stitch that looked like an angry frown. My short rows, requiring me to purl back, appeared misshapen, like a long scar. And here and there in the *lice* pattern that made up the bottom half of the Setesdal body, some of those single white flecks amidst the black were hidden from view, too tightly knit and looking like shy or embarrassed cousins of the proud black stitches. I despaired.

When I gave my wife a detailed tour of my knitting, she waved off my concerns. "It's only your first project. Don't worry—you'll get better."

That didn't help any.

Also, I hadn't told her (because I assumed she knew): This was going to be my *only* knitting project. I needed only one sweater, so why would I continue knitting when— and *if*—I finished? She was a true knitter; I was just making a sweater. And thus, I wanted my sweater to be perfect. As much as I dreaded the thought, I was ready to rip again.

My wife caught my hand and calmly took my knitting away. She stretched the knitted fibers horizontally and vertically, and then handed it back to me. It was a miracle performed right before my eyes: My knitting now looked decent, the plasticity of the stitch loops reorganized into neat marching steps.

Moral: As long as it doesn't unravel, you're doing just fine.

Lesson 6
If All Else Fails . . .

In the end, knitting those 46,080 stitches—plus another 19,200-odd stitches for each of the drop-shoulder arms—did not take me into the next decade. Time passed and the rows grew without pain or even much effort.

Then came the big day. I knit the collar, sewed the arms into place, and added the pewter clasps to the cardigan's front. I was ready to try my new sweater on.

The result was bittersweet. I was

Gauge, Gauge, Gauge Knitting Lesson: Proper gauge is next to godliness.

thrilled with my knitted fabric: The Setesdal pattern looked striking in stark black and white. Yet the fit left something to be desired. The belly had room for a paunch to grow into. One arm was longer than the other, although that could be solved by judiciously rolling the cuffs. The arms were downright baggy, as if they were to serve double-purpose as wings. The total effect of the sweater was akin to a misshapen potato sack.

My wife, however, was thrilled. She chirped as she danced around me, commenting on the beautiful pattern while tugging on the knitting to make the sweater stretch here and bunch up there.

When I pointed out that it simply didn't fit and was destined for the rag bag, she laughed and said, "Don't worry. You're not done yet."

The next step in knitting is "whapping," she explained. Filling our basement utility tub with water, she unceremoniously dumped my new sweater in the drink. She fished it back out, wrung it gently, then laid it on a towel spread over a tabletop. Without further ado, she began to beat my creation with a wooden yardstick. To my horror, I need hardly add.

"Whapping evens out the stitches and flattens the seams," she told me over the sound of beating my sweater was getting. "You'll see—it's almost magical!"

Sure enough, suddenly my uneven, unconfident stitches looked almost professional, even machine-made. Whapping was indeed a marvel.

"Now, we block it," my wife said, raising visions in my mind of her dropping concrete blocks on the sweater to further flatten it. This didn't seem a good idea, I was about to tell her, but instead she arranged my sweater on the tabletop, tucking in the sleeve waddles, bunching up one arm, and compacting the belly.

Now, I just had to be patient enough to wait for the wool to dry.

Moral: If all else fails, there's always blocking.

Lesson 7
Beware of Innocent Hobbies

If you look closely at my sweater, you can see every one of its flaws—uneven stitches here and there, too few short rows making the back ride high, and errors in the intricate Setesdal pattern. But to me, that sweater is a minor miracle. I made it.

When I first cajoled my wife into teaching me to knit, I had planned to stitch that one sweater and then quit knitting. But there was something I missed when I set aside those needles and yarn; knitting itself was almost magical. I found that I enjoyed the relaxation and craved the creation of knitting. Soon I began on a second project—a Setesdal sweater for my wife.

Nowadays, we both have knitting stashes, a shared collection of too many needles, and big plans for future projects that should keep us busy for years to come.

Moral: The only wrong way to knit is not to knit.

Dapper
Knitting lesson: Form follows function, but fit—and well-combed hair—is everything.

Chapter 2

Purls Before Swine
Infallible Excuses for Buying More Yarn

At one time or another, most every knitter is forced to come to the realization that they just might have more than enough yarn in their stash to last them through eternity—and perhaps beyond. Of course, this is usually not discouraging; it's just a minor epiphany on the way to spinning or buying another skein or two.

To help justify those next skeins—should they truly need justification—here are some excuses for putting purls before swine.

Yarn, Yarn, Yarn!
A cornucopia of yarn was available to eager knitters via mail order in these classic 1920s and 1930s magazine advertisements.

This color just might— someday—be discontinued

Stocking Up
A dapper gent admires this stylish knitter's baby—and her stash of skeins.

J. & P. COATS · CLARK'S **O.N.T.**

Everyone wears **SWEATERS**

Sweaters BOOK No. 291

10¢

CHADWICK'S RED HEART YARNS

Without all that yarn, your stock of knitting needles might get rusty.

Keeping the Needles Busy
There's nothing more embarrassing then rusty knitting needles.

You always need accent colors. And you always need main colors to accent.

Accent Colors and Main Colors
Which is which on these stylish tartan sweaters from the 1950s? Either way, you can never have enough color to play with.

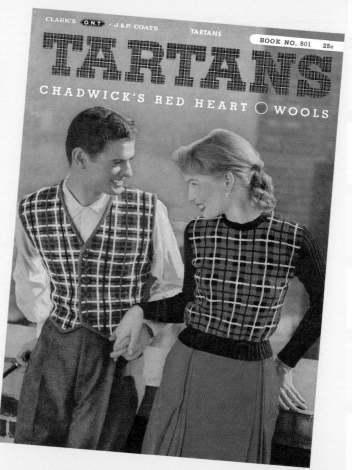

CLARK'S O.N.T · J.&P. COATS   TARTANS

BOOK NO. 501   25c

TARTANS
CHADWICK'S RED HEART ○ WOOLS

Best to stock up now in case there's a shortage.

Yarn For Free!

You could make your own yarn for nothing at home out of "run-damaged hosiery" and other throwaway fabrics with the amazing Webster Textile gizmo from this 1930s ad.

33

You don't have to cook it, dust it, scrub it, or vacuum it.

Low-Maintenance Textiles
There's no time for housework anyway when you have knitting on the mind.

Yarn stashes insulate the house.

Planning For Cold Weather

You can never have enough insulation when winter arrives.

It's illegal to steal it.

Don't Even Think Of Stealing It! Like two sides of one conscience, knitters gaze lustfully at a yarn display.

New
WOOL
BOOK

BOOK W-1   25 CENTS

SKIRTS   BLOUSES
BABY SETS   SWEATERS
AFGHANS   BEDJACKETS
SOCKS   MITTENS

Dawn AND *Clover Leaf* WOOLS

To support sheep ranchers.

Supporting the Farmers
Farming and ranching are tough businesses and they need your help.

Just one more skein can't hurt.

Never Enough Yarn
A fashionable knitter in her new red top shows off her skein stash.

You'll save gas buying bulk now, rather than driving back and forth to the shop again later because you know you'll buy it anyway.

Sweaters, Sweaters Everywhere!
If you have a hankering for sweaters, you *need* that yarn.

It's less expensive than therapy.

Joy!
Nothing brings a grin like a new winter sweater.

MEN'S and WOMEN'S HAND KNIT

WINTER SPORT *fashions*

of **BEAR BRAND** and **FLEISHER Yarns**

No. 735
(See Page 3)

VOL. 38 - 50¢

Yarn's not fattening.

Happiness
Happiness is a nice skein of a low-fat cashmere-wool blend.

10 Uses for All Those Extra Needles You Thought You Needed

(1) Back scratchers

(2) Toothpicks

(3) Chopsticks

(4) Hair holders

(5) Tent stakes

(6) Garden markers

(7) Fondue forks

(8) Kabob skewers

(9) Outboard motor shear pins

(10) Magic wands

Chapter 3

Patron Saints of Knitting

Apostles of the Divine Mystery of Yarn

— — — — — — — — — — — — — — — — — — — —

Mention the name "Elizabeth Zimmermann" to most folk and you'll be rewarded with a blank stare. Mention her name to a knitter and you'll be blown over with a tirade of tribute, a testimonial for her books, a warm personal anecdote, or all three. Zimmermann is one of knitting's best known and most beloved patron saints.

Knitting has other patron saints as well, although few of them are famous to the world at large. Perhaps that's because knitting is a craft lacking in romance and glamour, taken for granted as one of grandma's hobbies. By everyone but knitters, that is.

Without further ado, here then are some of spinning and knitting's other patron saints.

— — — — — — — — — — — — — —

Grandma

To most knitters, their own grandmother was their teacher, advisor, and inspiration.

Barbara Pym: Patron Saint of Knit Wit

In *Some Tame Gazelle*, first published in 1950, British author Barbara Pym wrote the Great Knitting Novel. The simple story revolves around two spinster sisters and their not-so-subtle war to win the hearts of two country clergymen with their superior knitting skills. Only Pym's wit could graft the knitting of socks and sweaters into a rich plot of secretive intrigue and open combat worthy of Jane Austen.

Edith Piaf: Patron Saint of Simplicity

Known as "The Little Sparrow," French chanteuse Edith Piaf sang torch songs of raw, heart-rending emotion. Befitting her persona, her stage "costume" was a simple black dress that she professed to have knit herself—although much about her life was in fact melodramatic charade. Yet whether Piaf knit her dress or not, she certainly crocheted the simple white collar that was the sole adornment and "color."

Molly Weasley: Patron Saint of Effortless Knitting

Only Molly Weasley could make knitting look so easy it must be magic. In J. K. Rowling's Harry Potter series, Mrs. Weasley's magical needles knit all by themselves in the family's bizarre home, The Burrow. Even so, the sweaters she makes are the stuff of family legend for their odd fit and scratchy wool.

Honorable mention goes to Mary Poppins, the flying nanny in P. L. Travers's books. While Mary's needles aren't magical, the mysterious satchel bag in which she carries her knitting certainly is!

Edith Piaf:
Patron Saint of
Simplicity

Jacques Plante: Patron Saint of the Manly Art of Knitting

Princess Eliza: Patron Saint of the Salvation of Knitting

Princess Eliza of Hans Christian Andersen's fairy tale "The Wild Swans" from 1838 has eleven princely brothers who have been turned into swans by their wicked stepmother. Seeking to break the enchantment, Eliza knits them shirts made of nettles.

Jacques Plante: Patron Saint of the Manly Art of Knitting

Ask most hockey players who their favorite knitter is and they'll answer "Jacques Plante." In fact, the all-star goaltender is likely the sole knitter most hockey fans know—beyond their own grandmas, that is. Growing up in poverty, Plante not only was forced to make his own first goalie pads from stuffed potato sacks, but had to knit his own jersey and tuque. Playing for the Montréal Canadiens, he found that knitting was relaxing and so knit hats and sweaters in the locker room and on the bench while leading the team to a record five consecutive Stanley Cups from 1956 to 1960. Bad enough that he knit, but after being hit in the face with a puck too many times, Plante was one of several goalies who first wore a mask to tend the nets. Both his mask and his knitting forced Plante to endure many a taunt about his manhood, although his record on the ice won him a slot in the hockey hall of fame.

Honorable mention goes to football player Rosie Greer, legendary for crocheting on the bench in between taking the field as part of the Los Angeles Rams' Fearsome Foursome.

Madame Thérèse Defarge: Patron Saint of Knitting Revolutionaries

Thérèse Defarge found a novel use for knits and purls. In Charles Dickens's 1859 novel *A Tale of Two Cities*, Madame Defarge, wife of a wineshop keeper with revolutionary leanings, calmly knits a registry of the names and crimes of those among the aristocracy whose heads should go under the guillotine. Knitting "with the steadfastness of fate," she's among those who storm the Bastille, her knitting set aside and a knife tucked in her girdle. As her husband says of her—with more than a bit of wariness in his voice, perhaps—"It would be easier for the weakest poltroon that lives, to erase himself from existence, than to erase one letter of his name or crimes from the knitted register of Madame Defarge."

Eleanor Roosevelt: Patron Saint of Knitting for Causes

"Behind every great man is a great woman," a popular saying goes, but Eleanor Roosevelt may have proved the inverse, that behind every great woman is a great man. Raised to respect a woman's traditional roles as wife and mother, she also saw beyond them to become an outspoken advocate of civil rights, workers' rights, and women's rights. She fought for affordable childcare and other support for woman entering the workforce during World Wars I and II. But it was her love of knitting that led her on one of her most famous missions, organizing knitting projects through the Red Cross to inspire homefront knitters to knit bandages for wounded soldiers. As she once said in tart retort to the world's expectations of womanhood in those times, "I could not at any age be content to take my place in a corner by the fireside and simply look on."

Glenn Miller: Patron Saint of Knitting Rhythm

During World Wars I and II when knitting bandages for the wounded was a wartime necessity, numerous songs were recorded honoring the homefront knitters. Some of the tunes were sentimental love songs, bearing titles such as "Knit a Kiss, Purl a Prayer." Others were straight-forward propaganda pieces, like "Knit for Victory." Still others were swing numbers with a rhythm ideal for knitting, including "Stick to Your Knittin', Kitten" and "Knit, Sister, Knit." The most famous was bandleader Glenn Miller's "Knit One, Purl Two" from 1942, a jazzy jump tune with the wistful lyrics:

Knit one, purl two,
This sweater, my darling, is for you
While vigil you're keeping through
    rain and storm
This sweater will keep you warm.
Purl two, knit one,
Our trials I know have begun
And while you are fighting each
    battle through
My darling, my heart's with you!

Glenn Miller: Patron Saint of Knitting Rhythm

Morticia: Patron Saint of Knitting Curiosities

Morticia was the matriarch of Charles Addams's infamous cartoon clan, the *Addams Family,* a dark-humored look at how the other *other* half lives. Whether it was gardening with Venus flytraps, interior decorating all in black, or playing dirges on her harp, Morticia was the antithesis of the suburban housewife. When it came to knitting, she was often seen in both cartoons and the family's movie debut at work stitching and purling a three-legged suit.

Holly Golightly: Patron Saint of Knitting Errors

In the film version of *Breakfast at Tiffany's* from 1960, Audrey Hepburn's Holly Golightly was the personification of hip—although she was also part runaway rube and part sad actor in a life lived at too quick a pace. For Holly, knitting was hip, although more than a bit confusing; her attention span ran to a jazz beat and her life was one long party. As she laments over her knitting project, "José brought up the blueprints for a new ranch house . . . I have this strange feeling that the blueprints and the knitting instructions got switched. I may be knitting a ranch house."

Ma: Patron Saint of Knitting Comfort

Both Aunt Bea of TV's *The Andy Griffith Show* and Harriet Nelson of *Ozzie and Harriet* were classic knitters, but it was Ma in *The Little House on the Prairie* books who was the quintessential knitting mother. Laura remembered the comfort induced by watching Ma knit by firelight in the evening, her needles flashing golden in the dark.

Miss Marple: Patron Saint of Unraveling

Whenever you're forced to rip, stop for a moment and think of Miss Marple, Agatha Christie's knitting detective famous for unraveling murders and mysteries. For Miss Marple, knitting was in truth a disguise, camouflage to hide behind and put evil-doers at ease while she calmly uncovered their plots with all the care that went into knitting a jumper.

First Lady Grace Coolidge: Patron Saint of Relaxation and Rejuvenation

A First Lady is all too often eclipsed by her husband's role, yet Calvin Coolidge's wife Grace was a power behind the presidency. While he was shy, she was outgoing; when he faltered in wielding his will, she was firm. She moved from being a well-educated New England housewife into the center of Washington politics and society, and as the President summed up their marriage in his *Autobiography*, "For almost a quarter of a century she was borne with my infirmities, and I have rejoiced in her graces." From Grace Coolidge's point of view, however, the infirmities of her position were a trial, and knitting—among other "woman's work"—kept her sane. As she confessed in the 1920s while she was First Lady, "Many a time when I have to hold myself firmly, I have taken up my needle. It might be a sewing needle, knitting needles, or a crochet hook—whatever its form or purposes, it often proved to be the needle of the compass, keeping me to the course."

Miss Marple:
Patron Saint
of Unraveling

Sirdar

No. 1332
'MAJESTIC' 3-PLY
Bust 38 inches
6ᴰ

Chapter 4

Knitting Affirmations
Reasons to Start New Projects
(Without Finishing Old Ones)

Knitters see UFOs everywhere. This isn't part of any conspiracy theory, but can be a sign of advanced knitting obsession. "UFO" stands for "unfinished object," a polite euphemism for the sweater, socks, mittens, scarves, shawls, and more that you started with all good intentions but just haven't managed to finish . . . yet.

Here are several reasons to allow your eye to stray from your current project to that new one that's simply too alluring to resist.

Another Reason to Start a New Project
Fashion always keeps you on the move.

A new shade of color caught your eye.

Pretty in Pink
If your mood changes from dark to bright, it's time to start anew.

J. & P. COATS • CLARK'S **O·N·T**   SWEATERS   BOOK No. 504   **25¢**

SWEATERS
For the Family

CHADWICK'S RED ❤ HEART YARNS

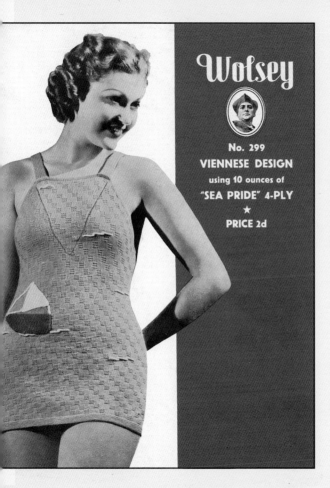

Wolsey

No. 299
VIENNESE DESIGN
using 10 ounces of
"SEA PRIDE" 4-PLY
★
PRICE 2d

The sun came out and you're no longer in the mood for that dark brown Icelandic sweater.

Bathing Time

When summer is on the way and you run across the perfect knitted swimsuit pattern, you simply must drop everything.

It's more fun and less painful than ripping.

Stylish Sweaters
Keeping up with the others at tea time can make for a strict knitting
schedule.

The green is always greener in that new dye lot.

Swank
Glamour depends on getting that color right.

Fashion trends changed from zig-zag multi-colored shawls.

Looking Cool
When the hippie look went out, it was time to look ahead.

Your no-stress project proved too stressless and you need something more exciting.

Stressfree
Excitement is just the thing for others.

Your no-stress project proved too stressful and you need something easier.

Stressful
Stress is not good for some knitters.

The child your sweater was intended for is now a teenager and no longer likes the teddy-bear intarsia design.

They Grow Up So Fast
Sometimes your knitting simply can't keep pace!

PATONS & BALDWINS'
SPECIALTY
'P&B' Knitting 'P&B'
BRAND   BRAND
Book
Nº 44

TWELVE
PRACTICAL
DESIGNS
FOR
TODDLERS
6ᴅ

Chapter 5
Knitting Disasters
Garments of Torture on the
Path to Perfection

By Sigrid Arnott

We all have skeletons hidden away in our knitting baskets—
those knitting projects that somehow went awry. Knitter
and fabric artist Sigrid Arnott here shines light into the
darkest corners of her needlework past and with wry humor
explains the lessons she hopes she learned.

Knitting Disaster in the Making
Warning: Multi-tasking can lead
to dropped stitches.

Like most knitters, the first thing I knit was a scarf. It was perfect.

I was a student in Italy and needed a scarf and gloves in a coppery rust color to match my tweed winter coat. In the small town where I lived, knitted items from gloves to lingerie were sold along with handknitting supplies in a tiny, quasi-subterranean shop. Basically, if it involved the knit stitch—whether factory fabricated or handknit—they sold it. After stepping down into the store, I faced a glass case of knitted accessories presided over by a gnome-like *signora* who guarded the contents as if they were priceless jewels. She selected an appropriate pair of gloves for me, but lacked a scarf that matched.

"Why don't you knit one?" she suggested. "I have just the yarn."

The fact that I didn't know how to knit didn't worry me, but it seemed problematic that there was no yarn in sight. American shops encourage customers to wander past wanton walls of yarn that tempt us to make imprudent purchases. In Italy, the yarn shop ladies would never allow such foolish behavior. The *signora* walked over to her wall of yarn—shelves of tightly closed boxes and hermetically sealed plastic bags—climbed a ladder and pulled down a single box. She carefully open it for me and awaited my approval: Inside were skeins of glorious mohair yarn in the perfect color. I didn't actually even see any other yarn or inquire about more economical possibilities. She tallied up the gloves, two skeins, a pair of needles, and sent me on my way.

Fortunately, my friend Lucia had been educated in a Waldorf school and knew all sorts of esoteric skills, including knitting. After spending months trying to conjugate unfamiliar Italian verbs, learning to knit was a breeze. Even so, by the time I actually finished my scarf, spring had arrived, and I was wearing a jean jacket and fixing fence back home in Montana. Yet the scarf was perfect, inspiring me to greater knitting glory.

In truth, all I had done was knit a large garter-stitch rectangle out of a beautiful fuzzy yarn that hid my uneven stitching. Even so, I now felt like a knitter. And in the United States, no *signora* controlled my access to fiber. Acquiring yarn became a hands-on experience as I fingered wools in fancy boutiques, comparison shopped at Ben Franklin, and greedily dug through my mom's stash.

At the same time, a dangerous book fell into my eager hands. Shocking as it may sound, I attribute many of my early disasters to knitting's *Grande Dame*, Elizabeth Zimmermann. Before I even knew what I was doing, I felt emboldened to design my own knits, to trust myself, to "unvent" with yarns that no LYS lady would have advised and no Italian *signora* permitted.

This conspiracy of coincidences led to a slew of disastrous creations. From the nicknames my garments elicited, it may sound as though I was doing contract work for an S & M shop. But at least I learned from my mistakes.

**Left:
The Power of
Purls**
Warning:
Simple can be
effective—
sometimes too
effective.

**Facing page:
Dressed For
Success**
Warning: Less
can be more,
especially when
it's revealing in
all the right
places. But
more can also
work—as long as
it doesn't make
suitors dizzy.

The Hair Shirt

From some chunky wools in various colors that I salvaged from my mom's stash, I knit a toddler's version of the modular tomten jacket shown in Zimmermann's *Knitting Without Tears*. My version was well executed: it looked great and fit fine.

Unfortunately, the blue that surrounded the torso was made from an extremely coarse, handspun Greek yarn that must have been made from minimally processed goat hair—with thistles still clinging onto the strands. Only a penitent monk, and certainly not a fussy toddler, could have endured the itching it provoked. I sadly christened my sweater The Hair Shirt.

From The Hair Shirt, I learned there is more than gauge to knitting a garment. You must also want to wear the fabric you create one stitch at a time.

The Hair Shirt

The Chain-Link Fence

Next, I decided to make a vest for my boyfriend. He was very definite in his color choice: the only yarn I could find in the deep hunter green color he desired knit up at about six stitches to the inch. Being a special guy, he scorned plain stockinette stitch and favored a complex basket-weave pattern he spotted in a

72

Cowboy Cardigan
Warning: For little cowpokes, being able to move your arms for the quick draw can be a matter of life and death.

knitting encyclopedia. The pattern was intricate and required my constant attention. It was also time-consuming—and seemed never-ending.

From The Chain-Link Fence, I learned that one must enjoy—*really* enjoy—stitching a fine-gauge textured pattern if you want to complete a boyfriend-sized garment. I didn't finish it, but we did stay together.

The Straitjacket

When I became pregnant, my knitting went into overdrive, and I completed two baby sweaters for a small financial investment at Woolworths. I remembered my lesson from The Hair Shirt and knit the first sweater, a cabled cardigan, from a soft, fluffy acrylic yarn.

I proudly squeezed my first-born into his brand-new homemade sweater, then stood back to admire my handiwork—only to watch in horror as he struggled even to move his arms. He thrashed about almost panic-stricken, but his little arms were held immobilized, stiffly akimbo. Then he burst out screaming.

From the few seconds I spent watching my son try to escape The Straitjacket, I learned that cheap acrylic yarn can become absolutely inflexible when knit in a tightly cabled design.

The Straitjacket

The Shackles

Chastened by The Straitjacket, I chose a natural fiber for my son's replacement sweater, a cotton designed for dishcloths. Although the resulting sweater was flexible, I bound off the wrists too tightly, which threatened to cut the circulation of blood from my infant's chubby little fists.

From The Shackles, I learned to bind off lo-o-o-osely, especially when using yarn with the flexibility of cotton string.

The Sweater of Shame

My next disaster was close to a masterpiece. But not close enough.

During a particularly grim Minnesota winter, I worked at a discouraging job in one of those futuristic, environmentally friendly underground office buildings that was in truth perpetually cold and damp—and ultimately, depressing. As I spent long hours in my cave working at a computer using anti-ergonomic, pre-electronic office equipment salvaged from an abandoned World War II Veteran's Administration psych hospital, I developed pains in my hand that were diagnosed as carpal-tunnel syndrome. Yet, as an anodyne to my job, my knitting obsession was at a peak.

Although it hurt to knit, I loved working on my knitting project. I designed a Norwegian-style sweater with floral patterns knit in colors that I borrowed from a glowing Turkish sock. Shocking pink flowers flowed from apple-green leaves over a blue background. The pattern and colors of the garment were the antithesis of my workplace.

When I first wore my new creation, I believe I blinded my co-workers (appropriately clad in mole-like browns and black) as I traversed the dank maze of subterranean offices with large neon flowers rioting across my body. Now, when I pull the depression-busting sweater out of storage each fall, I feel retro-active shame that I even wore it out of the house.

From The Sweater of Shame, I learned that the saturated colors I love will glow when carefully set against a larger dark background, but when used with abandon as both design element *and* main color, they just create a crass competition for attention.

I also learned that although you can wear just about any brilliant color, bold pattern, or bizarre creation on your feet, adult-sized sweaters require more finesse.

The Sweater of Shame

SMART

Knitting

AND NEEDLECRAFT

70
original
designs for
family and home

NEW FEATURES

★ things to make
  in one night

★ complete
  beginners
  section

SMART KNITTING'S OWN ANGORA ARGYLL
Instructions on page 56

35 CENTS

**Big, Bold,
and Beautiful**
Warning:
Sometimes
restraint is
rewarding.

Planning for Future Disasters

Undeterred, I happily continued knitting with faith in the future. I gifted my far-flung family with my amazing knits, so I'm positive there were other garments of torture that I unwittingly created and they were too polite to mention—The Thumb-Screw Mittens, The Iron Maiden Hat, The Stocks Socks, and one particularly memorable Scarf of Self-Flagellation. Maybe these garments helped my family and friends cast away their bodily concerns, feel penitent for their errors, and ponder the divine. It's more likely the knitwear ended up in the trash.

Of course, it doesn't help that, although I have thousands of patterns at my disposal, I have never once purchased the recommended yarn and followed the full directions for a garment. As time went on, though, I got it right more often than wrong. Still, although I learn from my mistakes, there remains an infinite number of ways that I can screw up. I envision knitted ideals, glorious in their perfection, but the translation from heavenly vision to earthly reality sometimes results in abomination.

The odd thing is that my disasters never discourage me. I retain the optimism I had as a knitting novice walking out of that Italian shop with my first skeins of yarn ready to make that perfect scarf. I vow never to be a crabby crafter, my enthusiasm jaded by seeing one project too many end in calamity. Instead, I imagine my next perfect project, cast on, and enjoy the ride. My oeuvre of disasters is large but represents little more than my desire to create gone just wrong enough to fashion a botched version of my ideal.

Someday, though, it will all come together—the yarn, the design, the fit, the colors, the architecture—and I will know that all the disasters I created along the way were, in their strange and ugly forms, required stops along the way to a masterpiece.

It will be the consummation of my aspirations.

It will be perfect.

because a little piece of yourself goes into everything you knit...

Knit Wig
Warning: A <u>lot</u> of yourself goes into everything you knit.

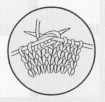

Chapter 6
Purls of Wisdom
Warning Signs That Your Knitting Controls You

To say that knitting is an obsession with most knitters is stating the obvious. In fact, "obsession" sometimes seems a rather mild description.

Here are some warning signs that you are knitting obsessed—although you may already recognize several of these in your own life and not even care.

Secret Knitter
Knitting in school broke the teacher's rule.

You look at your dog or cat and think of all that good fiber just going to waste.

Feline Furball and Canine Skeins
Turning cat or dog fur into yarn has crossed many a knitter's mind at one time or another.

gay *Teen* ideas

for knitting and crocheting

You take "mental health" days off from work to re-organize your stash.

"Spare Hours?"
If only there were spare hours so you could knit more!

84

You can't openly bring more yarn into your own home due to family "issues" but have to resort to subterfuge to infiltrate new skeins.

Knitting Secret Agent
Sneaking more knitting supplies into the house sometimes requires deft under-cover work.

You try to spin yarn from dryer lint.

Looking Good
Only you will ever know.

FLEISHER'S

TWO PIECE VESTEE DRESS
No. 2333
Directions on Page 52

HAND KNIT APPAREL
*for Sports
Travel
Town Wear*
VOL·37
25¢ (IN U.S.A)

You teach your seven-year-old how to knit— starting with intarsia.

Starting Young
A simple swatch is just the beginning.

You spend more on yarn, needles, and notions than on food.

Bare Necessities
Sometimes you have to hock everything you own for more yarn.

MINERVA
KNITTING BOOK

VOLUME XXIII

PRICE 25¢

Your idea of relaxation is working on your intarsia sweater project with its sixty-four shades of color.

Style is Everything
For some knitters, the more colors and the more complication, the better.

Your idea of a dream vacation is a fiber-gathering mission to the corners of the globe to select a yak fleece on the hoof.

L'AUVERGNE PITTORESQUE
98. - Tricoteuse Auvergnate

Knitting Postcards

What better way to say howdy to the folks back home while on your knitting expedition than postcards of fellow needleworkers?

Your family members can't safely sit down anywhere in your house without getting poked by knitting needles.

Sitting and Knitting in Comfort
With so many needles, how are you supposed to remember where they all are anyway?

You insist on doing it all yourself—from raising your own sheep to spinning your own wool—just for a new pair of knit socks.

"Saa sulla ho Mor Paa Rokken sin"

Photo by A. T. Hagen

Assembly Line
And there's dying and felting to think about too.

You take language courses to learn Latvian so you can translate sock patterns.

Going Native
Latvian is only the beginning; there's also Finnish and Aymara to master.

You're secretly sure that you can knit a sweater row faster than a **NASCAR** driver can lap the Daytona speedway.

Speed isn't Everything . . .
But it's sure fun!

You dream of finding a way to knit while you drive your car.

Making Up for Wasted Time

If only you could put all that wasted time sitting at stoplights to good use. And then there are those highway straight-aways where hands on the steering wheel are not essential!